Huntu !

#BeeInspired
Practical Steps For Living A Life Full Of Joy

Thanking God for my Mom & Our Legacy.

BEE SMITH

Swiner Publishing

DURHAM, NORTH CAROLINA

Bee Smith

(405) 808-4599

9713 Essex Ct.

Swiner Publishing
Durham, North Carolina /27703
http://www.docswiner.com

#BeeInspired / Benedria D. Smith – 1st ed.
ISBN **978-1540743657**

#BeeInspired / Benedria D. Smith – 2nd ed.
ISBN **978-1-948752-17-6**

I dedicate this book to the following:
The Hurting
The Rejected
The Different
Who Feel Not Worthy
Not Enough
Too Fat
Too Skinny
Too Smart
Too Ugly
Too Dumb
Too Ambitious
Too Much of a Dreamer
The Loser
The Abused
The Abuser
Those Who Feel Unworthy of Love
Those who feel their dreams are too BIG, but they are too
Small!
The Lost
The Stuck
Those Who No Longer Desire to Live in this Realm

—BEE SMITH

CONTENTS

ABOUT THE AUTHOR

Benedria "Bee" Smith is the Giver of Useful Information. That Inspires! She Is a Humanitarian of the 21st Century! An Multi-International Best-Selling Author, Public Speaker, Multi Media Personality, and Publisher. Well known for her dynamic personality and high-impact presentations, she is a tireless community advocate, spokesperson and educator.

She passionately serves as a Suicide Prevention and Mental Health Advocate using her experiences as a beacon of hope for those battling mental illness. She serves as Media/Communications Specialist for her local Chapter of the American Foundation for Suicide Prevention.

She is the Creator #BeeInspiredTalks, an event focused on the Depression and Suicide Awareness including and up to prevention measures, bringing hope and light to those suffering in silence. You can catch her on both local and national TV and Livestream segments offering commentary with a joyful smile and captivating energy!

DR. TINA THOMPSON

FOREWARD

Few elements of the lived experience are so common everyone is familiar. Light is universal. Its purpose, use, and comfort are familiar. So familiar, in fact, that without its existence many experience suffrage. Benedria (Bee) Darcel Smith exemplifies light. Her aura is influential, magical, and indistinguishably purposeful. Her soul is one she shares, one to provide comfort and one to elicit love.

I first met Bee while traveling to Chile on an international learning experience. Both Bee and I were learners pursuing our doctoral degrees. Little did I know, I was inviting that light into my life at our introduction thousands of miles away from home, since our original meeting, we have spent countless hours in conversation and shared experiences.
Early did I observe her passion about life and recognized a lasting connection had been made. Helen Keller states, "Character cannot be developed in ease and quiet. Only through experience of trial and suffering can the soul be strengthened, ambition inspired, and success achieved."

Through a series of life experiences, Bee has grown to know pain, defeat, loss, and scarring. Her ability to overcome challenges and utilize the strength and fortitude she has gained from past trials is inspiring to witness.

Her character is a representation of a multitude of meaningful experiences, loss, grief, fears all transformed into strength, confidence, and magnificence.

This book design is as an expression of Bee's life in her words. She has an incredible ability to demonstrate how living a purposeful, passionate life can occur despite experiencing some of the most challenging experiences know to human beings.

Bee is a master at finding value within herself and details how she has come to exude such confidence. She shares her remarkable gifts and illustrates in literature how to identify these same gifts within ourselves.
She also shares how helping others is an extension of the gratitude in which we all maintain the call to live in this state consistently. As a fellow learner, scholar, and girlfriend I give witness to the compelling story shared within this book. May possibly you see the strength, gifts, and talents that lie within Bee but also within ourselves.

May you receive the love and share with our fellow army of beautiful women. May possibly you find layers of value within yourself. May you identify the gifts you have within yourself that are designed to be shared and love given to others. May your life experience positive transformation by reading this book but most of all inspired by the journey Bee has so bravely shared.

Tina Thompson, DBA

Admirer and lifelong friend

CHAPTER ONE

DIRECTIONS PLEASE?

When planning an excursion into an unfamiliar location of interest, a Global Positioning System serves as an effective guide. I just love my GPS when I need to get to a specific place, especially if I am running a little behind. Every move is perfect. No worries. The GPS converses a specific time at which you will arrive. Now that is awesome sauce! Too bad life does not come with a GPS. Things would be perfect! Think about it: you would never have to wonder if you made a bad decision. Of course, life also would be pretty darn boring, but at least we would never get lost.

Personal thinking is that my direction has always been the opposite of the norm. I always knew I was different. GPS would have been great to have in the fall of 1979 when Mrs. Dobson, my kindergarten teacher at Dewey Elementary gave me those dreaded green scissors that were difficult for lefties to use. Go figure. It already took me forever to write my name and oh, those darn blisters on my middle finger because I was determined to write like the other 90% of the population! To this day, if you look at my perfectly manicured hands you can detect a soft callus on my left middle finger, but at least I do not write like the typical left-handed person. My penmanship is neat as can be! You will frequently catch me joking that I was destined to be a smart cookie—I had to learn how to spell my name! These labels or marks of who we are begin early in life. As children, we take these labels to heart because that is all we know to do, and they often carry into adulthood. How else does a seven-foot man walk around the neighborhood answering to Peewee? Sheesh! Adults should truly consider that there is more in a name. Not only was my name difficult to pronounce and spell, but my nickname was worse: Stinker-Boo. Really? Who came up with that? My big brother, go figure that I would be my siblings first to torture victim! My family thought it was cute so it stuck. I would claim to be the first Boo, but then I would have to divulge the entire middle name to receive copyrights. So, not going to happen. One dirty diaper and the name follows me forever. What can I say? The legacy of shame began early.

THE SPOTLIGHT

If you desire the spotlight, being the second of five children is NOT the pace to get it. Of course, each child in the family hierarchy receives a label. My label was "the smart one" or the one least likely to do something stupid. To this day, I am not sure if this was a natural part of my personality or if it was my way to fade into the abyss undetected. Personal thinking during my formative years was that if I made good grades, kept my dress clean and my hair in the proper place, I would be okay. I remember reading book after book and daydreaming of flying, but in most of my daydreams, I would imagine myself being invisible and flying around undetected. I remember feeling small until it was time to play.

One of my favorite games as a child was follow the leader. In this game, the players line up behind the leader and imitate his or her moves. Players who fail to follow the leader are out of the game. The last player standing is the new leader. In life, personal thinking is that the leader is the last one standing. From elementary to middle school I would excel in scholastics, the arts, and pretty much anything outside the home I could get myself involved in. I recall co-writing a screenplay for the history fair in the sixth grade. The "Great Wall" received numerous awards and recognition in the Oklahoma City History Fair. We won so many awards that then governor George Nigh requested we perform during the state Senate session!

For once in my life, I stepped into the spotlight and let my artistic light shine. I recall being so happy and in my element, experiencing a part of the world only seen in my dreams. Even with attempts to stay in my fantasy world where I was invisible and fade into the scene of mediocrity, the natural leader in me would come out.

Bee the leader would face life in all of its intricacies, trips and turns, emerging from the dreamer to the believer. Surviving suicide in 2009 changed my personal lens on life and living in a new way. Life is not perfect, but I am full of joy. No longer do I dread waking up, but I look forward to a new day. I no longer hide from the sun, but I smile to feel its warmth on my face. This journey has given me a love for God's best creation: people. I love people and their perfect imperfections, which make them unique. The purpose of this book is to encourage others through my journey to see life in a different lens. A personal lens, one whose intent is to uncover the inspiration to live purposeful and in abundance of joy, using individual gifts and talents to be the change you wish to see, and last, but most important, live HAPPY and full of JOY!

CHAPTER ONE REFLECTIONS

CHAPTER ONE REFLECTIONS

CHAPTER TWO

THE GROWTH FACTOR

Before we get to rainbows, unicorns, and all things joy, I must share with you the experience that propelled me into the ball of inspiration I am today. When your growth helps others to grow, all one can do is reflect, smile, and appreciate. You see, no one wants to reveal the life dirt, because it is just that: dirt. One important thing about dirt is that it has a reason for existing. Its purpose is to support growth. Only in uncovering our dirt, sharing our experiences with others and watering it with personal truth, can the beautiful plant that is our life's path flourish and grow.

Well, I have always been a leader, but this time, I did NOT lead successfully with regard to suicide because I woke up. Well, sort of. One thing I remember so clearly is the voices all over my head while in the emergency room. I remember the nurses directing my husband from the room as they began work on my weary body.

I felt as if I was having one of those out of body experiences. Unable to move, but very aware of my surroundings. I remember tears falling from my face but for some reason I felt no need to wipe them. My life began to flash before my eyes.

There was no white light, but images of events passed. My mother's face, my dad picking me up. Me playing with my cousin Tamika in my grandmother's high heels, my first kiss, then my babies...my babies. None of the horrible things that ended me up in this cold, surgical place entered my thoughts.

For once, all the negative images, thoughts, and emotions that ruled my existence for months, and even seemed liked years, were no more.

No worries concerning the job, others' opinions, my waistline, the length of my hair or the way I talk. None of those things we take so seriously for whatever reason or another. Life in this spectrum was full of laughter, light, and appreciation. Then silence and a peace like no other. No sadness. No pain (a shocker, as physical pain was all I had known for the last six months).

There was nothing. I felt like air. Almost as if I could fly. This was cool except for the fact I could not move. That part really freaked me out, and then there was calm. In that moment, I began to communicate with God.

I remember our conversation clearly. It was as if he and I were watching a movie and I was the star! Go figure! Of course, I am always talking, so this day was no different. I said, "God if you take me today in spite of my actions, I know you forgive me and I will be with you." That is all I remember.

God is so forgiving, because those BIG eyes that I used to be embarrassed for others to see opened up. I made a promise before I closed my eyes that if those eyes were blessed to see another day that I would LIVE. Moreover, live aloud and drive in my OWN lane! I would respect the roadmap for my life. You see, my personal roadmap is the experiences, people, places, and lives I have a chance to touch each day. No GPS needed. Just an appreciation for the trips and turns that comes with this life. Without those turns, I would never have gained the clarity and peace that I have today.

I was one of those people, living in discontent and lacking appreciation for those lessons of life. Instead of using those turns as opportunities, I was angry for making human mistakes, not realizing mistakes are a part of growth.

Sometimes a wrong turn turns out to be the best direction. My consistent advice is to take fear and throw it out the window! Never be afraid to take the path of least resistance. It is the road less taken because it is the road specifically for you. No one is there, because it is YOUR path. If we neglect our paths, we leave others without the light to discover their paths. Our walk is the light that shines to guide those who inhabit this space long after we leave this life. This life is not our own, but we as humanitarians are here to help one another along the way.

When I walk into a classroom, lecture hall, television station, or podcast interview, I share this knowledge with listeners/viewers, detailing triumph, loss, change management, and the importance of following those playground goals, or the dreams and aspirations we had in the beginning. Even in kindergarten, I wanted to be a teacher. I took a few turns along the way, but those bumps in the road make me the best professor ever. I get an overwhelming sense of joy when I see the engagement and comprehension that dreams are for fruition, not deferment!

Each day is another opportunity to empower, inform, and encourage someone else. I am fortunate to share my experiences and learn from others how to navigate through this life in gratitude. I have met and interacted with humans all over the globe sharing the vision of Positive Imagination. This journey, while not perfect, is rewarding. I consider my life not my own, but to share hope and humanity with others. You see, it was only when I could imagine a better life, could those images change. Dreams are the initiation of our ideal reality. In the next chapter, we will examine a four-step process to living a life full of joy.

CHAPTER 2 REFLECTIONS

CHAPTER THREE

DREAM. PLAN. EXECUTE. REPEAT.

DREAM.

The first step in this process begins with a dream. A series of thoughts, images, and sensations occurring in our time of rest and recharge. Dreams are but a glimpse of life's possibilities. So vivid in color, but so real in the mind. In dreams, the unthinkable is possible. No limits. No travel delays or baggage claim receipts to collect, only the dream in perfect design. Faith is the confidence of things longed for, the confirmation of things not seen. As a child, I remember vivid dreams of flying to Africa or snorkeling in the Great Barrier Reef off the northeastern coast of Australia, as well as the countless hours reading books and thoughts of traveling to South America to feel the sun on my face.

Attempting to explain these visions to my grandmother in our small town of Fort Worth, Texas proved futile, as she would smile and politely hand me another book and some crossword puzzles to keep my eventful mind occupied. I share this story because at some point all have dreams.

Those thoughts are powerful, so do not discount them. Maybe you will never fly like Peter Pan, or be the Invisible Man, but these thoughts in our dreams are the foundations of one's personal life roadmap. A plan for the future.

PLAN.

Even with all of the education and accomplishments gained during my 40-plus years of life, my most profound memories of my present life come from my playground plans. Personal thinking is that our draft life plans come from birth, and in our childhood, we clearly comprehend what our lifework on earth should be. As an elementary student I recall telling my friends, "I want to be a doctor and a teacher," in the most profound manner. My friends would laugh and say, "Blood is gross!" or "You want to cut people up!" and I would reply that my desire was to be a doctor who studied the mind through books.

Of course, this did not win me too many friends in elementary, middle, or high school. Throughout my teen years, these plans remained stifled by family struggles, lack of self-love and rejection. These struggles shaped personal views of self-worth and took me away from the vision the creator had of me. Every quirky detail, from my left-handed self, to my love of books and crazy thoughts for changing the world, intricately designed for my purpose by God, remained hidden in an effort to gain acceptance from a world who did not comprehend. I know now that I was out of alignment of my dream. Back to the original plan. Dream it. Plan it. Now Execute!

EXECUTE.

Fast-forward execution of this perfect life plan includes heart-break, mistakes, loss, grief, fails, wins, setbacks, illness, numerous degrees, and a host of life experiences that would send anyone packing back to the dream phase. In our dreams, we are safe; we wake up just before the doom hits. Do you ever recall a dream that was so awesome, you did not want to wake up? Everything seems so effortless and put-together. Until you wake up. In real life, we are very awake to feel the joy, pain, and other mix of experiences life offers us as humans.

I lost my way. I decided that I would deviate from the perfect plan and be what others thought I should be. I was good with numbers, so my life path was deviated for more than five years, driving the other accountants crazy with my bubbly personality. This aspect is critical to share as I had realized that God had a perfect plan for my life in which I would not have to attempt to be what others suggested, but walk in purpose, naturally using personal gifts and talents for "thoughts of peace, and not of evil, to give you an expected end" of success (Jeremiah 29:11).

Execution of one's life purpose is far from perfect, but successful when eloquently aligned in the will of God. When we operate in his will, we comprehend that our creator has supreme confidence and confirmation in our abilities to serve the universe. What does that mean? It means you are important. It means that you have a place, a skillfully designed place in this world. It means there is work to do, and that in living your purpose, you help others to find their purpose. For many years, I allowed rejection, fear, others' opinions and lack-minded thinking to be a barrier to execution of this perfect plan for my life. Today, I am that aspiring doctor of the mind, a professor and world traveler who has felt the sun on her face in sunny South America, a lover of books, educating and mentoring the next level of world leaders. I practice a life once only in the experience of a dream. Dreams do come true. You must have confidence in the confirmation. The confirmation is deep in your heart. You can build a legacy and have a life of joy in the process. All things are possible when you believe. Dreams your dreams, write out a plan, and execute!

REPEAT.

Now the repeat phase of the process is where things can get fuzzy for you, the audience, so I will make it clear. Many times in this personal journey, fear would thwart my goals, just short of my breakthrough. New journeys, new levels, higher heights, and deeper depths will continue to exist. To the readers of this book, I ask you to believe in the confidence and confirmation of your life process and know that one success is just a stepping-stone to your next level of excellence. Use fear as an engine—NOT a brake—and keep pushing. Trust me. It is not the end, only the beginning.

As long as you are breathing, there is work to do. For those who have arrived and no longer require personal growth, you can take your wings and go to glory. Those of us who are still learning and growing need the space on earth. Personal development is a life-long process in which we learn more about personal thinking about ourselves, and how we view the world. This expansion is not only beneficial to you the learner, but to all those in which you encounter on your journey in life. You become a beneficial member of the human race, helping others along the journey. Every day I caution you to put your execution on repeat. Go deeper. Do good stuff in the process.

Keep living a life full of joy!

CHAPTER 3 REFLECTIONS

CHAPTER FOUR

IT'S A PROCESS

Did the change happen overnight? Nah, it took some time to put it all together. Besides, the plan was for me to be dead. Death was to be my escape from life, people, and its challenges. Because I woke up, it was time for a new plan! Since I yet breathe, I knew in my heart there HAD to be a purpose. Where does one go from here? The peace I felt was so comforting. How do I find this on earth, with people's opinions, judgment, social class, and other personal issues of life? During my therapy sessions, the practitioner often spoke of transformation. According to Macmillan, transformation is a change into someone or something completely different, or the process by which this happens (MacMillan, 2016).

Transforming one's life journey requires multiple phases of growth. In the remaining sections, we will discuss the following topics: Stinking Thinking, Forgiveness, Service, and Purpose. These four key topics encompass the necessary mindset adjustments to live a life of wealth, joy, and abundance.

STINIKING THINKING.

Mindset is critical to initiate change. This type of change helps individuals to become masters of personal everyday life and long-term development (Oettingen, 2012, p. 1). To experience effective long-term development in any area, one must access their level of thinking. What do you see? What are you speaking? Better yet, what are your expectations? Getting to a life full of joy requires a joyful way of thinking. In this section, we examine three critical steps to rid the mind of negative chatter that robs us wealth, joy, and abundance.

There were so many times I would catch myself thinking the worst in situations. I talked myself out of opportunities that were staring me directly in the face. My mind was so prepared for negative reactions that these types of situations became the norm. No wonder I was so depressed. That is why in this section we are going to take out the mind-poop and clean up the stinking thinking! The true power to turn things around and live a purposeful life is in our thoughts.

How inspiring is it to know that the power we seek in others was inside of ourselves the entire time! Just imagine using our thought powers like an action hero! Instead of looking to an action figure for inspiration, we could merely look in the mirror, hold our head up and see our own reflection of power.

I can vision it now: It's a Bird, It's a Plane...No It's Me Fixing My Own Damn Life! Taking responsibility for personal thoughts and actions. No longer blaming others, while at the same time, taking my destiny into my own custody. Under-standing the power was mine all the time! Okay, now that we are all revved up and dressed up like our favorite superhero (in our minds, of course), let us get on with some useful infor-mation to rid ourselves of that dirty self-talk that needs to go to laundry. In #BeeInspired, I introduce what I call the *Bee-Atti-tudes* for living the life you deserve.

STEP ONE: BEE ONE TO MEDITATE.

The practice of meditation, philosophical or operational, is an "act of spiritual contemplation" (Perez-De-Albeniz & Holmes, 2000, p. 49). For me, meditation is a peaceful time. A time of day that I do not give to anyone else. Sometimes I may sit in my car for a few minutes before lecture. Sometimes I may stay in the shower an extra five minutes. Whatever the situation, I make sure to begin my day with some spiritual contemplation.

During the years I was depressed, I gave so much to everyone else that by the end of the day I was exhausted and had little time to consider truly taking care of me. Personal thoughts were of the kids, the house, etc. Did my husband have his lunch packed for work? More importantly, did someone remember to put the clothes in the dryer? Seems funny, but these were pri-orities! With all of my perfect Stepford Wife abilities, I found no time to reconnect with me.

To meditate is a treat. I feel like I am gifting myself clarity. Clarity is key to sound, productive thinking. If your thinking is stinking, it is probably because you are all over the place and not allowing your mind some much needed quiet time. Just think, if you practice this each day, you have more to share with others. You fill your cup daily, and then go sprinkle your happy juice all over the place! Simply put, you need to find a quiet spot, clear your head, and give yourself a chance to think clearly. People ask me all the time how I keep such a positive disposition. I tell them I meditate. Even the worst problems do not seem so bad after you have taken a few moments to breathe.

Once you have taken a few moments to breathe, you can look at the issues of life in a new way. Think for the best. How do you wish to see your relationships, employment, education, and your life plans? When I was 304 pounds, one of my first visions while meditating was of me running.

I opened my eyes in shock! For one thing, I could barely walk two blocks. How in the heck was I supposed to run? For the next few months, I continued to meditate (to help with anxiety) each day before leaving the house. I appreciated the calmness it afforded me. My moods were more stable, and I gained laser-focused skills to get things done.

Today at over 100+ pounds lost, I have a regular running regimen, and I meet with like-minded individuals who keep me motivated. To think this all began with a vision of me running while performing meditation. This is a clear personal example of advice imitating life, for the better.

Ridding yourself of stinking thinking requires personal accountability and practice. Once you begin to form the habit of clearing your schedule for YOU, it easily becomes part of your daily routine. Who knows, you just may develop a habit that improves your life in ways your cluttered mind would have never imagined.

STEP TWO: BEE INTENTIONAL

The second step to changing your mindset to a more positive disposition is to set intentional actions. What are you thinking and speaking? How is your lens or view of the world affecting your actions? In my personal lens, I see a future full of life, health, wealth, and possibilities. What do you see? As you, begin to clear your mind, gain new perspective. Living with depression, I was barely making it day-to-day. I just let life happen. The idea of a plan was far from personal view. You see, when we just allow life to happen you negate the universe's ability to conspire to bring you wealth.

For example, when I was planning the book launch party for *Fabulous New Life: Volume 2*, I had a clear, direct plan to donate 100 books to survivors of suicide at a local event. I was ecstatic because I had an investor who had agreed to donate the funding to purchase the books. Long story short, the donor experienced financial difficulties and was unable to deliver the funds as promised. I was devastated. Funds were tight at this time in my life, I was in the middle of family struggles, and it seemed that my clear plan of action to gift books to the patrons was to be an epic fail!

To make matters worse, my contracts for personal business were low, meaning there were no additional funds for me to use to purchase the donated books. In my heart, I knew gifting the books was the right thing to do. I begin to meditate and remember the clear and intentional action I had written in my plan. I spoke positive affirmations over my action plan. *I will donate these books. I will budget and I will have enough funds to make it financially with my business.* While on vacation in New Mexico, it seemed that all was lost. Still holding on to my positivity and faith, the subject of things hoped for and the evidence of the unseen.

That same day I received a text from one of my business partners asking if I was available for an additional contract to instruct a business course. You should have seen me dancing across that hotel floor in New Mexico! Wealth in action! Even better, my friends and I decided to visit the local casino and check out the nightlife. Happy with my new contract, it was time to let loose and enjoy the evening. I sat at a slot machine or two and won $60, then lost $20, but it was fun playing from the winnings. I had to be sensible, as I *was* on a budget. Toward the end of the night, I sat at a random slot machine as my friend gathered the remainder of the team.

Next thing I knew, the slot machine was lighting up like Christmas in April, literally! I had won enough money to enjoy the remainder of my trip, pay fees, AND purchase the books for the suicide survivors. Oh my! I had practiced the art of keeping my focus on my intentional actions and maintaining faith, even in the face of letdowns, and this was the result!

It may not have come the way I had initially planned, but I experienced the universe supplying me with wealth to complete the task set forth in the intentional action. Come on universe! Now that is inspiration personified through setting intentional action! It is not effective for me to ask you to perform an action. This is my book, so I choose to share my personal experiences with you to offer evidence of personal thinking and results. Besides, you have millions of gurus and experts who can give personal philosophy on this or that topic, but how about some empirical life examples of practice that bear fruit you can chew on. Okay, why not? Thought so. Let us move on to our third step in getting a life!

STEP THREE: BEE GRATEFUL

The third step in getting rid of that funky, stinking thinking is to live simply with an attitude of gratitude. For every hard luck story, letdown, or less than stellar experience I could share, there is someone on this earth, who has experienced that and a million times worse. Have you ever just sat outside on a sunny day and looked at our beautiful world? On a sunny day, the sky is clear, there are no clouds, and it is a blue more beautiful than words can describe. Sunny days are easy to describe, but let us consider a cold day.

On a cold day, if you stand close to a window to look outside, you will see a fog. When I was a small girl, I used to love breathing on glass and making that pretty circle on the window. That beautiful circle made by the breath from my mouth. You see, we take for granted the gift of breathing, or life for that matter. If you watch the local news, you see story after story of those who pass from this life, as we know it. As the old folks used to say "life is but a vapor," and I truly understand that now. Those we love are here one day and gone the next. The life we know can be gone in a second.

Now I am not judging, because I am no different. For many years of my adult life, I wanted to die. I never felt worthy. Not pretty enough. I had a pretty face but a thick waist. I thought surely the universe made a mistake, because how in the world could a human maintain such a profound disconnect from the world I lived in. I felt like an outsider who never truly fit in anywhere. It always seemed that the world was going right and I was swinging a hard left.

Today, I view those differences in a new way. Beating to my own drum is what makes me unique. The experiences I had, good or bad make me who I am. Learning to appreciate nature helped me to appreciate that I am apart of all things living. It is my divine nature. As you awaken to your divine nature, you will begin to appreciate beauty in everything you see, touch, and experience (Dyer, W, 2012). Choose gratefulness each day. Never forgot how beautiful it is to exist.

To live. To love. To experience this sometimes complicated, but always a beautiful life.

Getting back to and appreciating nature is the first step in learning to live a new way! Of course, this does not happen overnight. Changing ones mindset is similar to reprogramming a computer. It takes work and consistent practice to begin a new way of living life. A life full of joy and appreciation.

For so long I lived a double life. One in public, and a painful existence in private. However, today things are different. I am an advocate. A voice for the Voiceless. Totally LIT (Living in Truth)! I used to be Silent because I was Afraid no one would care what I had to Say. I used to hesitate because I was afraid I would fail. You are just like me; experiencing life and our persona grow and mature with every life circumstance.

No longer afraid, I accept every good seed that grows in my life and so should you. Each time, I share my story; it lets me know that my voice is powerful. Someone needs my light. Someone needs me to keep pushing. Purpose is the ultimate gift to every living person on this earth. Therefore, I ask, Who Is Waiting on You. On the other hand, maybe the question is what is holding you back.

CHAPTER 4 REFLECTIONS

CHAPTER FIVE

FORGIVING FORWARD

Forgiveness is the most powerful thing you can do for your physiology and your spirituality, and it remains one of the least attractive things to us, largely because personal egos rule so unequivocally (Dyer, 1999). I believe that life is like the seasons. We have spring, summer, winter, and fall. In the spring, nature is full of beauty, untainted by the harsh elements. Even when it rains, it leaves behind a sweet smell of the flowers, and sometimes you even catch a rainbow.

Such a forgiving season, that even after everything gets all wet, the beauty reappears. Pretty amazing, huh? The four seasons, as different as they are, work together to provide life source for the earth. I in turn practice four steps to forgiveness and living an abundant life full of joy!

STEP ONE: BEE FREE

Research states that the practice of forgiveness reduces anger, hurt, depression and stress, and leads to greater feelings of hope, peace, compassion and self-confidence. Committed forgiveness leads to healthy relationships as well as physical and mental health. This commitment opens the heart to kindness, beauty, and love. Does that mean forget the trauma that we experience? Of course not, but what it does mean is that to live a full life, one must comprehend exactly how one feels about the experience and what about the experience or situation is not okay.

Next, have a trusted person or group people in your circle in which you can share your experiences. For me, this was my therapist and a few members in my group therapy session after the suicide attempt and resurgence of childhood issues. The last step to becoming free is to make a personal commitment to yourself to do what you have to do feel restored.

Forgiveness does not necessarily mean reconciliation with the person that hurt you, or condoning the unfavorable actions of others. The end goal is peace. Peace is that freedom. We must use each experience that disturbs our peace, learn from it, and protect our peace as if our life depends on it!

STEP TWO: BEE REFLECTIVE

Reflection is a powerful tool concerning personal commitment to forgiveness. Looking back is only good if you are moving forward. Dealing with past hurts, misunderstandings, bad relationships, and love lost can be powerful if you use these memories in an effective way. I had to gain the right perspective on what was happening in my life and past events. Recognize that your primary distress is coming from your hurt feelings, thoughts and physical distress of the suffrage, not the offense or hurt you experienced five minutes—or ten years—ago. Forgiveness helps to heal those hurt feelings. Reflection is merely a reminder that you made it! When I think about the fact that my eyes opened and I could see my family again, my heart begins to sing.

In my mind, I recall the overwhelming desire to make the pain go away. Life was too much. The pain, the despair. The misunderstandings. The lack of comprehending my value to this earth. All a big misunderstanding. To think, my voice forever silent. No more memories. No more experiences. No more Bee. No #BeeInspired. My negative perception of life during the time originated from hanging on to undesirable emotions, hurt feelings, and some poor personal choices of the past.

Instead of reflecting on experiences as building blocks for success, I focused on the failure point of view in my thinking. During the process of forgiving others, you must first commit to forgiving yourself. Whoever started this idea of perfection truly screwed up our thinking concerning personal value, sheesh! For goodness sake, give yourself grace and understand that we all make mistakes.

Mistakes are opportunities to get better, to grow, to live a full life! Once you master the mistakes that took you back, you know better how to move forward. You will make better choices in your daily life; you will make better decisions in who you choose to allow in your space.

Last, you will gain deeper insight into what makes you uniquely you. You will learn to be okay with you. You will attract those who appreciate the real you, mistakes and all. Bee-lieve me, the freedom that comes with a village in which you can fully walk in your purpose is irreplaceable. The journey to joy is daunting, but not without some bottlenecks. Becoming an Author is something I wanted to do since I was six years old. At times, life happened and it was tough. I recall times I had to really pull on my faith and determination.

I had to say "I Believe" in everything my creator says about me, not others. I had to change my focus! I share this to say if you listen to what the naysayers believe, then you will miss the opportunity to deliver your message to the world in your unique way. If you let one or even ten fails for that matter or any type of rejection stop you, then you will never win. I have never seen a winner quit. I think it is because they simply do NOT know how. Good days or bad days, I will remain grateful, humble, and persist!

Persistence takes resilience through reflection on wins, losses, and everything in the middle. The next section deals with flexing that resilient muscle on our purpose.

STEP THREE: BEE RESILIENT

Mistakes give you muscle. I remember watching the cartoon *Popeye* as a child. Each time the main character Popeye would get into a situation he could not handle, he went straight for his spinach. Shortly after taking in the spinach, his muscles would visibly grow. You could see the passion and confidence in his face. He would use this strength to handle the situation.

What I appreciate most about this series is that at the end of each episode, Popeye would move on with life. There is a powerful message in resilience here. Troubles come, but we must reflect on what makes us strong and use it to our advantage. This means placing your energy into considering another way to acquire your positive goals and objectives than through the experience that was hurtful or damaging to you.

Instead of mentally replaying the experience, seek out new ways to get what you want and be the victor, not the victim. As I reflect upon the suicide attempt, it was merely an escape from my problems, not a solution.

Resilience in forgiveness comes from letting go of our stinking thinking about who and what we are, and understanding that we all make mistakes and this is a part of life necessary for personal development and growth.

Second is the realization that everyone has value. My mother would frequently remind me as a child to never feel like I "was better" than anyone else. Dignity and respect is a requirement to every living thing in humanity.

Comprehension of my personal value was the catalyst in my new thinking. Those quirky details of who Benedria was and is. These are qualities. Not faults. When you begin to comprehend and appreciate that you are as valuable to the universe as dirt is to the earth and making things grow, you will truly appreciate your presence in the present.

Think about the power of dirt. It is not pretty, sometimes it does not smell very good, but with water, some sun, and time, the planted seed produces fruit.

The power to live a full life resides in our present, NOT our past. When you look at a beautiful flower, you see a beautiful flower, not the dirt from whence it came. Living in the now. The moment. Embracing all that life has to offer in those precious seasons of life. Appreciation of the present is the key to the pursuit of personal purpose.

I truly believe in my heart that we connect to the universe in unity. With this unity, each living being has a purpose for existence. There is a passion in each of us that we or anyone else around us may not even comprehend. Once you find your purpose, joy is abundant.

CHAPTER FIVE REFLECTIONS

JOY ON PURPOSE

For me, purpose is the meaning of life! Without purpose, we experience a form of disconnect from all things which surround us. I often hear people asking "What is my purpose?" or "What is the meaning of life?" and it makes me ponder why we have to find something that we have connection to in the first place. Finding purpose is like finding that $5 bill tucked in your old jeans two days before payday.

No really, it feels that good. Maybe even better than that. What I wish to convey is that when one considers value, or in this case personal value, the impact of purpose is great. Now finding your purpose is not always so clear. Sometimes our purpose is just like that $5 we thought we lost, but come to find out; it was with us the entire time. What a revelation! Tucked away and hidden from plain sight, a treasure waiting to rise to the surface and be useful.

When speaking to my mentees, students, or business professionals, I often say, "Pinpoint your passion. Pursue your purpose," concerning direction in action. Why? I believe that comprehension of personal value bears a distinct connection to a personal sense of purpose. Some describe life without purpose as a tragedy (Munroe, 1992, p. 5).

My purpose saves me from tragedy. I agree. Imagine a life without purpose. That would be similar to going on a long trip in the middle of nowhere without a compass, a map, a GPS! Now that is a tragic story if I ever heard one. Reminds me of a funny excursion while traveling one spring in New Mexico.

A few of my world traveling friends and I were visiting some historical monuments in the United States while knocking a few states off of our "we have done it" bucket list. With clear action plans (and a GPS), we headed to the Four Corners Monument to experience the Quad-State areas of Utah, Colorado, New Mexico, and Arizona. Then we moved on to a peak named Shiprock. *Shiprock* is a monadnock rising nearly 1,583 feet above the high-desert plain of the Navajo Nation in San Juan County, New Mexico. Its peak elevation is 7,177 feet above sea level. I still recall visioning its beauty from hundreds of miles away.

With such beautiful descriptions, it makes it simple to comprehend why this monadnock would be on our list of areas to travel. As we traveled the rugged rural area to gain access, it began more and more difficult to reach Shiprock. We began to lose direction. The GPS went nuts. Then the road ended. It just ended. We could only get so close to it. To be safe, we just had to stand back and marvel at its beauty.

We were a bit frustrated that we could not get closer, but excited that we took the precautions and stopped when we reached the peak of the destination. It is amazing how we think we want something. We want it so bad, we are willing to do whatever it takes to accomplish that goal or reach that destination. However, what if that is not the purposeful destination for you? I share so you can comprehend that in pursuit of your purpose, you may run into a dead end, but that does not mean it is the end.

Sometimes you must stand back and experience the beauty of how far you have come. When I think about my story, and how I survived, my purpose calls me to share. Share with others my pain, loss, depression, and feelings of helplessness. Telling my story prevents me from using the past as a crutch. I understand that bumps in the road happen, and we have to overcome to get to our purposeful destinations. They are not a stopping point, but they exist as an opportunity to give one a moment to plan action for the next step.

My purpose is like finding $5 in those old jeans. Was life over because I lost a five-dollar bill? No. Did it suck to lose some cash? Yes. This example illustrates that just because we lose in one area, not all is lost. When I was in my deepest depression, I would endure a loss in one area of my life and my stinking thinking would have me all in my negative feelings that my ENTIRE life was over. One incident does NOT cancel out your purpose. Sometimes things, situations, and people in our lives are simply misplaced. Not to mention these losses or misplacements usually teach us something we can use later.
Just like that $5. No telling how long it was in my pocket, but I assure you as soon as I got my hands on it, I spent it! I promise you I am cracking up at myself as I share this knowledge nugget with you. You must seek the unseen benefit in every situation.

Learning to laugh at our personal experiences is necessary to live and look at life with a healthy lens or perspective concerning our life work.

Purpose gives you a sense of humor. You begin to look at life in a new way. There is less exaltation of perfection and more expectation of fulfillment! The cool thing about purpose is that we all have one. Our lives touch other human beings in ways unimaginable to commonality. We sit back looking at someone else thinking how freaking awesome they are, when someone is looking at us in the same manner.

Think about it for a second. The hair industry makes billions of dollars each year in marketing/product sales. People with curly hair buy products to straighten their hair. Those with straight hair walk around with curlers, rollers, and hair treatments to get that perfect wave/curl pattern. Perfection sucks you in and steals your joy. Acceptance and appreciation would make life simpler in the scheme of things, for sure.

In summary of all things purposeful, hair, dollar bills, and trips to the middle of nowhere without a map, GPS, or compass, I desire for you to find YOUR purpose. This treasure belongs to only you. It lives inside of you. It never leaves you. It is your sense of being. It is what you do without even trying. It is your gift to the universe. A gift that fills you up in the darkest moments of your life. Your purpose reminds you why you exist. An interchangeable, required, needed element of the universe. We are helpers of one another with the simple element of thriving in our gifts and simply being who we are. When I was younger, I experienced much teasing about talking so much.

Friends and family would say, "Do you ever run out of things to say?" and, I am almost sure I had some form of response.

Talking is my thing. You see, my linguistic nature is my gift! My purpose is to be the giver of useful information. I exercise my purpose in my teaching, mentoring, encouraging, sharing my ups and my downs, in my educating and training future leaders to be the best in all they do!

In review of purpose, we must pinpoint your passion! Find that thing about you that drives everyone nuts, but in turn draws people to you. It is something on the inside. An organic enthusiastic response. A unique gift that only you can provide to the universe. This allows you to live in your truth.

You will make better decisions in work, play, and relationships. This form of kinetic energy is contagious, affording you a joyful, abundant, and wealthy life. Passion will catapult you to rise to the occasion even when you do not feel like it. The passion placed in our DNA, a recipe pre-constructed with instructions to complete a mission only we can uniquely perform.

I truly appreciate operating in my purpose! Purpose is the one thing that helps me to maintain a consistent joyful disposition in all situations, even in the tough times. I understand that the issues of life are temporary.
I choose joy and to take a lesson from each experience. Think about it. Why go through something and fail to learn from it. I reflect on the weight lifting from past mistakes each time I share a lesson learned that encourages and gives hope. It may not have felt good at the time, but the knowledge gained

strengthens me for the next level. I can take that dirt, put a little water on it, and wait for the beautiful flower to grow.

One last lesson on purpose I wish to share with you is profound. In this spectacular journey, the discovery that what others believe about your purpose is absolutely, positively, indubitably, in No way, shape, or form, ANY of YOUR business! Keep the Faith. Keep Working. Keep Believing! Ignore the Noise. Mind Your Vision from Above and Do the Work!

CHAPTER SIX REFLECTIONS

CHAPTER SIX REFLECTIONS

JOY IN SERVICE

Although this is the final piece in this offering on personal philosophy of living a life full of joy, wealth, and abundance, this is a critical step in preserving our purposeful nature. I totally find the humanitarian aspect of life fulfilling. You look at the world outside of yourself. You possess empathy and compassion towards your fellow man with acts of service. Before we discuss service, we must examine the act of humanitarianism. A humanitarian is one concerned with or seeking to promote human welfare (Oxford University Press, 2014). Thus, when we find our purpose, it is natural to use our gifts helping others. Service is the act of the action of helping or doing labor for someone.

Giving to others is the best form of healing. Each time I have the honor to walk into a lecture hall and give instruction, mentor youth, advise business professionals, or even share my story of survival with a stranger at the local coffee shop, it reminds me of how far I have come in personal development. When I first began to volunteer, I was so ashamed and fearful of what others would think of me, but I assure you that each time I share and help someone else, that fear and shame goes away. With each walk I participate in, each lecture, each therapy session, I feel empowered by being an overcomer. I remember those humanitarians who reached out to me in my time of loss. The therapist that used their skills to teach me coping techniques. The members of my group therapy who lived in their truths, sharing with me that they had struggles, too!

GET LOST IN SERVICE

Much of the time, most of us feel that we are alone in our respective situations. Acts of service places us with others who not only understand our situation, but strong bonds form because of participation in these acts. You begin to glean and share new tools. It reminds me of the pay-it-forward type of ritual. If I can stop one suicide and get one youth to comprehend personal value in the face of others disapproval, I feel a sense of joy.

You can find this joy, too. Participate in local community and non-profit organizations.

For example, my younger brother Zachary L. Colbert was born prematurely in 1980. Because of his premature birth, he came to this earth with underdeveloped lungs and a hole in his heart, rendering him mentally and physically challenged for his entire 24 years of life.

I recall a local March of Dimes (MOD) organization who had rallied around my family. They would deliver information to my family from the time my brother was born through various representatives, volunteers, and state agencies. I recall volunteers helping my siblings and me help my parents to care for my brother as a family unit.

Each year they would have an annual walk in my city. It was amazing. There were people from everywhere at the walks and so many other children who looked like my brother. Other families, who were different but just like mine. I remember smiles, laughs, and a feeling of accomplishment as we completed the walks as a family.

Today, I serve as a lifelong volunteer and board member for this great organization. I never hesitate to use my platform as a public speaker to volunteer and encourage other families to serve our communities.

SERVICE REFLECTIONS

This life journey indeed comes with challenges, but the power to an abundant life of joy come with service to others. It catapults a "boomerang effect" and the joy comes right back. I consider myself blessed to share personal/professional knowledge with others. Getting lost is service saves you from repeating past mistakes.

You gain new direction. I knew that when my eyes opened my life was no longer my own. I recall the service of each medical professional involved in saving a life. My life. Now I must share the keys to fulfillment in life. Not a perfect life, but a life of wealth, joy, and abundance.

As I reflect over my journey in this life, I can only smile. Each heartbreak, loss, relationship, and experience make me who I am. I dream, plan, execute and repeat daily. My lack of perfection just means I live another day. I am reflective of the sum of my experiences in life.

I appreciate each season as it occurs; living in gratitude with every breath, I take. This book is so far from perfect, but it is real. My life is real. Your life is real. My life is necessary. Your life is necessary. We are unique contributions to the universe. The universe needs us.

My desire is to live a legacy that will pour into the universe long after my mortal existence is complete in this realm. This is my service. My purpose. My inspiration. BeeInspired.

CHAPTER SEVEN REFLECTIONS

CHAPTER SEVEN REFLECTIONS

EPILOUGUE

Merriam-Webster (2016) states that an epilogue is "a concluding section that rounds out the design of a literary work". The purpose of this work has been to inspire others to see the value of their lives through the individualities that they possess. Bee's gift in life is to bring that message to others by sharing her life experiences, and she does that with an inner light of joy and grace. To round this work out, I would ask you a question: Do you feel the joy? I have known Bee about 2 years, now, and she spreads joy and inspiration to every person she meets, so I know you feel it. That joy is included in the pages of this book, and you are now in possession of that gift. What will you do with it?

You chose to read this book because you already knew you were ready to fly. Now is the time to make that flight happen. Go and use Bee's inspiration to light that fire deep inside your being to propel you into action. Do what you KNOW you are here to do. Go! DO IT!!!!

Chanin Warren Rivenbark, MBA
Friend and Sister from Another Mister

ABOUT THE CONTRIBUTORS- FOREWARD

Dr. Tina Thompson
Independent Consultant – Owner Tina Thompson Consulting
Senior Academic Success Coach, Capella University

Dr. Thompson works in the higher education community working with learners, leaders, and organizations to maximize persistence and operational effectiveness. She has 18 years of experience as an educator, coach, and business leader.

Her professional background is founded in higher education, for-profit, non-profit, and government experiences. Her academic areas of specialty include leadership, business management, organization development/administration, strategy, and innovation.

In addition, Dr. Tina Thompson is a collaborator and consultant using research, experience, & knowledge to produce client specific results. Her consulting practice concentrates on authentic leadership, coaching, research, data collection, and data analysis.

Her research interests are in authentic leadership, organization development, employee retention, organizational commitment, and profitability.

Dr. Thompson has earned a Doctorate of Business Administration in Leadership from Capella University and an M.A. in Organizational Leadership from Gonzaga University. She has received her B.S. in Family Social Science from the University of Minnesota.

Contact information: tinathompsonconsulting@gmail.com or **1-651-246-1867 or** www.tinathompsonconsulting.com

ABOUT THE CONTRIBUTORS-EPILOGUE

Chanin Rivenbark BS, MBA, TOGAF Certified
IT Business Professional
Department of Defense

Chanin Rivenbark is a North Carolina native currently working in the IT field. She holds a BS in Materials Science and Engineering and a Certificate in Computer Science from NC State University, and a MBA from Capella University.

Chanin has had a diverse professional career serving as a Software Engineer, IT Support Technician, Chief Technology Officer, IT Architect, IT Manager, and Quilter/Artist. Chanin has experience in the private sector, public sector, and has owned her own small business.

Chanin spends most of her free time with her three teenaged boys, but also enjoys hiking, running, football, and travel. A few accomplishments that Chanin is particularly proud of include: visiting all 48 continental US States and 4 different continents, earning a Black Belt in Tae Kwon Do at the age of 40, and making friends wherever she goes.

REFERENCES

Dyer, W. (1999). *Manifest Your Destiny: The Nine Spiritual Principles for Getting Everything You Want.* New York City: Harper Paperbacks.

MacMillan. (2016). Transformation. In *MacMillan Dictionary*. Retrieved from http://www.macmillandictionary.com/us/dictionary/american/transformation

Merriam-Webster Dictionary. (2016). Epilogue. Retrieved from http://www.merriam-webster.com/dictionary/epilogue.

Munroe, M. (1992). *The Pursuit of Purpose.* Shippensburg, PA: Destiny Image Publishers.

Oettingen, G. (2012, March 1). Future thought and behavior change [Article]. *European review of social psychology,* 23(1), 1-63.

Oxford University Press. (2016). In *Humanitarian.* Oxford: Oxford Dictionaries.

Perez-De-Albeniz, A., & Holmes, J. (2000). Meditation: concepts, effects and uses in therapy []. *International Journal of* Psychotherapy, 5(1), 49-58. http://dx.doi.org/doi:10.1080/13569080050020263

Made in the USA
Middletown, DE
14 January 2020